THE SCIENCE BEHIND
NATURAL
DISASTERS

WILDFIRES

THE SCIENCE BEHIND RAGING INFERNOS

Dr. Alvin Silverstein, Virginia Silverstein,
and Laura Silverstein Nunn

Enslow Publishers, Inc.
40 Industrial Road
Box 398
Berkeley Heights, NJ 07922
USA

http://www.enslow.com

Library of Congress Cataloging-in-Publication Data:

Silverstein, Alvin.
    Wildfires : the science behind raging infernos / Alvin and Virginia Silverstein and Laura Silverstein Nunn.
        p. cm. — (The science behind natural disasters)
    Includes bibliographical references and index.
    Summary: "Examines the science behind wildfires, including what causes them, the different types of wildfires, their devastating effects, and how to stay safe during a wildfire"—Provided by publisher.
        ISBN-13: 978-0-7660-2973-6
        ISBN-10: 0-7660-2973-5
    1. Wildfires—Juvenile literature. I. Silverstein, Virginia B. II. Nunn, Laura Silverstein. III. Title.
        SD421.23.S54 2010
        634.9Ú'618—dc22
                                2008048025

Printed in the United States of America

10 9 8 7 6 5 4 3 2 1

♻ Enslow Publishers, Inc., is committed to printing our books on recycled paper. The paper in every book contains 10% to 30% post-consumer waste (PCW). The cover board on the outside of each book contains 100% PCW. Our goal is to do our part to help young people and the environment too!

To Our Readers:
We have done our best to make sure all Internet addresses in this book were active and appropriate when we went to press. However, the author and the publisher have no control over and assume no liability for the material available on those Internet sites or on other Web sites they may link to. Any comments or suggestions can be sent by e-mail to comments@enslow.com or to the address on the back cover.

Illustration Credits: Andrea Booher/ FEMA, p. 8; Associated Press, pp. 21, 36, 39, 42; David R. Frazier Photo Library, Inc./ Photo Researchers, Inc., p. 24; Mario Anzuoni/ Reuters/ Landov, p. 4; © Michael Rolands, Shutterstock®, p. 10; National Aeronautic and Space Administration (NASA), p. 34; National Aeronautic and Space Administration (NASA)/ MODIS Rapid Response, p. 6; © Owen Hugh Retief, Shutterstock®, p. 12; Paul M. Ross, Jr./ 911 Pictures, p. 19; Reuters/ Adam Tanner/ Landov, p. 9; Stephen & Donna O'Meara / Photo Researchers, Inc., p. 28; © Thomas Mounsey, Shutterstock®, p. 14; United States Geological Survey (USGS), pp. 18, 33; U.S. Bureau of Land Management, p. 27.

Cover Illustration: A wildfire in Quebec, Canada. Publiphoto/ Photo Researchers, Inc.

CONTENTS

AGUA DULCE BURNS

On October 21, 2007,

a ten-year-old boy was playing with matches in the back-yard of his home in Agua Dulce, a rural town in Los Angeles County, California. The weather in the town was hot and dry. In fact, Southern California was having one of the driest years on record. As the boy tossed the sizzling matches into the dry, rain-starved grass and brush, it didn't take long before small flames appeared.

Soon the flames grew bigger, and the Santa Ana winds helped spread the fire quickly. These winds were unbelievably power-ful, blowing at hurricane

> *** It's a Fact! ***
> Four out of five wildfires are caused by people.[1] The fourth leading cause of outdoor fires is children playing.[2]

A home burns in the Rancho Santa Fe area of San Diego, California, in October 2007.

speeds up to 161 kilometers (100 miles) per hour![3] By the time firefighters finally brought the fire under control, it had destroyed more than 38,000 acres and burned down twenty-one houses.[4] It was a wildfire—a rapidly spreading fire, usually in a wilderness or rural area. Unfortunately, this fire was only one of more than twenty wildfires that raged from Santa Barbara County to the United States–Mexico border during October 2007.

While the wildfires raged, hundreds of thousands of people in Southern California had to leave their homes. The fires destroyed hundreds of homes and businesses. A total of fourteen people died, but it could have been much worse.[5] An emergency

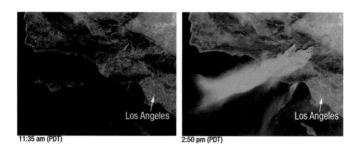

These satellite images show how rapidly the wildfires grew on October 21, 2007. The image on the left was taken at 11:35 A.M. and the one on the right was taken just over three hours later at 2:50 P.M. The smoke blowing off the coast in the later image shows the intensity of the winds as well as the presence of additional fires further south.

phone call system probably saved many lives. In addition, many people found out about the wildfires by watching the news coverage on TV.

People in the danger zones grabbed what they could and fled their homes. The highways were jammed. Some people went to stay with relatives or friends. Hotels filled up quickly, and emergency shelters were set up. Local stores ran out of water, food, and other basic supplies.

Thousands of firefighters worked hard to put out the

Why Are Wildfires So Common in Southern California?

Southern California has a lot of wildfires mainly because the climate is hot, dry, and windy. The powerful Santa Ana winds can turn a small wildfire into a huge, widespread disaster. These winds pass through narrow canyons, which increase their speed.

Santa Ana winds are very dry and warm. As they blow through Southern California, they suck up moisture from all the plant life in the area. Dry grasses and shrubs can catch fire very easily.

wildfires. But the fierce Santa Ana winds kept blowing. It was almost impossible to bring the fires under control. The winds finally died down about a week or so later. On November 9 the last fire was put out, about three weeks after the first one started.

Fire officials investigating the fires found a variety of causes. Some were accidental, such as the one started by the boy who

A firefighter works to control the Poomacha fire at the La Jolla, California, Indian Reservation in October 2007.

admitted to playing with matches. Fallen power lines, due to the strong winds, were blamed for another fire. But some of the fires were set on purpose. The police arrested a number of suspects. The causes of other fires were not known.

California's October 2007 wildfires became one of the worst wildfire outbreaks in United States history. The fires destroyed more than 500,000 acres and temporarily forced nearly 1 million people out of their homes.[6]

A man walks through the ruins of his former home after it was destroyed by wildfires that spread through California in October 2007.

WHAT IS FIRE?

Lighted candles flicker

on a birthday cake. A fire glows in the fireplace on a cold winter night. Flames shoot out of the windows of a burning house. Clouds of smoke rising from a wooded area may be signs of a hidden wildfire.

A tiny flame on a birthday candle and a huge wildfire sweeping through a forest are both fires. All fires— no matter what they look like—are basically the same. So what exactly is fire?

> *** It's a Fact! ***
> It can take less than thirty seconds for a small flame to get completely out of control and turn into a major fire.[1]

A cloud of black smoke rises from a burning barn.

How a Fire Starts

The ancient Greeks believed that fire was one of four basic building blocks that made up the world. The other three were earth, water, and air. Today's scientists know that's not true. Earth, water, and air are all forms of matter. Matter is anything that has weight and takes up space. This includes gases, liquids, and solids. But fire is not a form of matter. It is a process—a chemical reaction. When a fire burns, substances are changing into other substances. This reaction also releases heat.

A fire cannot burn without three important ingredients: oxygen, fuel, and heat. Together, they form the "fire triangle." Each side of the triangle represents one of the ingredients. It needs all three sides to stay a triangle. Take away any of them—oxygen, fuel, or heat—and the fire can no longer burn.

Oxygen is a gas. It makes up about 21 percent of the air we breathe. (A fire needs air that contains at least 16 percent oxygen.) The more oxygen a fire gets, the bigger and hotter it becomes. When oxygen combines with a fuel, the chemical reactions may be fast

Any fire needs these three ingredients to burn.

and violent, and the fuel starts burning. This burning is called combustion.

Anything that can burn is called fuel. Fire needs fuel to grow. Some materials burn more easily than others. That's because they can combine readily with oxygen. Paper and wood, for example, are very combustible, (able to burn). Other combustible materials include dry grass, coal, oil, and gasoline. Most metals will burn only at extremely high temperatures. However, heat can make them melt, or go from a solid to a liquid state. Some materials, such as ceramic tiles, are noncombustible. They will not burn at all because they do not react with oxygen.

Wood doesn't suddenly catch fire because it is surrounded by oxygen. It needs the third and last ingredient—heat—to get a chemical reaction going and start a fire. Heat can come from a number of things, including fire itself (such as a burning match), focused light (from the sun or a lightbulb), friction, lightning, or volcanic lava.

Words to Know

Another word for combustible is *flammable*. (Oddly enough, *inflammable* also means burning easily. The word *non-flammable* describes things that can't burn.) Materials that do not burn are also said to be fire retardant. Children's pajamas, made of flammable cloth, are treated with fire-retardant chemicals that keep fires from spreading. Many artificial Christmas trees are also fire-retardant.

Can Rubbing Two Sticks Together Really Start a Fire?

Yes, but it's not as easy as it looks on TV. When you rub two sticks together, you create friction. Friction is a force that generates heat. The rubbing action has to be fast, though. The sticks should be as dry as possible. Dry wood has a better chance of catching fire than wet wood. However, it takes a lot of patience and practice to start a fire by rubbing two sticks together. You need a very high temperature to start a fire. So friction can take a long time to generate enough heat to do the job.

It takes heat to start a fire, but fires also give off heat. As a fire burns, some of the chemical energy stored in the fuel is changed into heat energy. The heat produced by a fire helps keep the burning going.

Usually fires produce light as well. That is, some of the stored chemical energy is changed into light energy. The color of the light depends on how hot the fire is and also on what is burning. The hottest part of the flame, at the bottom, is a glowing blue. The upper parts of the flame glow orange or yellow.

The blue part of this Bunsen burner flame is the hottest; the red area is cooler. Bunsen burners are used in chemistry labs.

The Stages
of Fire

Fire goes through a number of stages. In the first stage, fuel must be heated to a very high temperature for a fire to start. This is called pre-heating. Different fuels burn at different temperatures. A sheet of paper, for example, is more combustible than a piece of wood. So the paper burns at a lower temperature than the wood. The temperature at which a fuel burns is called its ignition point. Ignition is the start of a fire.

The amount of moisture in the fuel can also affect ignition. Dry fuel burns faster and more effectively. So a dried-out log will burn better than a wet log.

The second stage of a fire is called flaming combustion. At the ignition point, materials in the fuel start to break down. They release flammable gases, along with tar, water, charcoal (almost pure carbon), and ash. Ash is a powdery gray substance that contains all the unburnable minerals in the fuel.

The flammable gases rise and mix with the oxygen in the air. These gases react, causing flames to appear. At this stage of the fire, the actual burning takes place in the gases above the fuel. In addition to the flame, the fire may produce smoke, a mixture of flammable gases and tiny carbon particles. Depending on how much carbon is mixed with the gases, the smoke may be light gray, dark gray, or even black.

How Can a Spark Make an Open Container of Gasoline Explode?

Gasoline is a liquid that can turn into a gas (vapor) very easily. In fact, at room temperature, some of the gasoline has already turned into a gas and mixed with the air above the liquid. Add a spark—from a cigarette lighter, for example—to that flammable gas mixture, and you get an explosion. For this reason, it is dangerous to smoke or light a match at a gas station or in a house with a gas leak.

In a fire's third and last stage, known as glowing combustion, the fuel itself burns. Some substances containing carbon, such as gasoline or heating oil, form only two products when they burn completely—water and carbon dioxide. Wood and other fuels may not burn completely, however. The fuel leftovers are called embers. They can continue to burn for days or even weeks after a fire has no more flames. A slow burning such as this is called smoldering.

UNDERSTANDING WILDFIRES

When early humans discovered

how to create fire, it changed their ways of living. Fire provided warmth, light, cooked food, and help in making tools. Now people were able to live in colder climates.

Heat is still an important source of energy today. We use it to warm our homes, cook our meals, and make appliances and machines work. But fire can become dangerous when it gets out of control. That's what happens in wildfires.

> *** It's a Fact! ***
> Under certain conditions, a wildfire can spread very quickly—up to about twenty-three kilometers (fourteen miles) per hour.

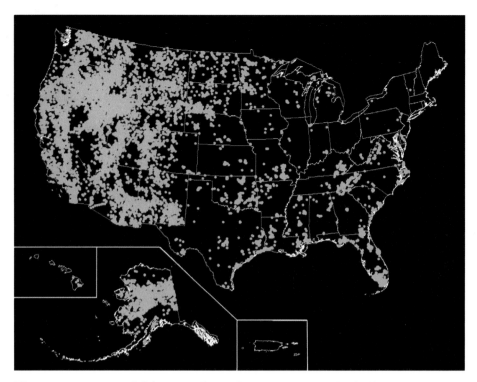

The orange areas of this map show the occurrence of wildfires that burned more than 250 acres between 1980 and 2003.

Weather and Wildfires

Wildfires are more common in some areas than others. A major reason is the weather. Wildfires are more likely to start and spread in a dry, hot climate, rather than one that is cool and rainy. Hot weather can help heat up burnable materials to their ignition point.

Rain can slow down wildfires. But storms can also start fires or help them spread. For example, thunderstorms produce lightning bolts. When a lightning bolt strikes a tree or house, the energy it carries can quickly ignite wood and other burnable materials.

Thunderstorms can also produce strong winds. These winds can help spread fires by carrying bits of burning material to new areas. They also fan the flames, bringing in more oxygen-filled air to keep the fire going.

Hot, dry weather and strong winds make a dangerous combination. Grasses, bushes, and trees dry out during long periods

A daytime wildfire moves along the ground through pine needles and underbrush.

without rain. These dried-out plants can be ignited very easily by a small flame or even just a spark. So any region that has long periods of dry weather has a high risk of wildfires.

How Do Wildfires Spread?

Wildfires can spread very easily through wooded areas. They will burn any combustible materials in their path. In fact, they can also spread to residential areas and burn houses, barns, and other buildings.

Fires spread by transferring heat energy from one object to another. This happens in three main ways: radiation, conduction, and convection.

Radiation. Heat from a fire spreads outward, or radiates, in all directions. But some of the heat energy is lost as the fire moves. So the farther a person is from a fire, the cooler it feels. The heat from a fire can ignite materials close to it. Generally, however, this heat will not ignite buildings more than nine meters (thirty feet) away from the fire.

Conduction. Heat from a fire can also pass through objects in direct contact with the fire. For example, if one end of a log ignites, heat travels quickly to the other end. Soon the whole log is burning. Burnable materials in the path of the fire, such as a field of dry grass, can carry—or conduct—heat and spread the flames.

Convection. Moving air can also spread heat from a fire. Heated air rises, and cool air falls to take its place. So the air around a fire is constantly moving. For example, heat travels upward from a fire that starts in the dry leaves and other dead materials on a forest floor. As it rises, this heat warms up the leaves and branches of the trees, drying them out and then igniting them. The moving air can also pick up burning materials and carry them to unburned areas far from the fire. These embers, also called firebrands, can start new fires. Convection can spread a wildfire much faster than either radiation or conduction.

Flames of a wildfire rise behind this South Dakota home in July 2006.

Do Mountains Slow Down Wildfires?

No. In fact, wildfires actually move faster when going uphill because heated air tends to rise. Fuels such as grass and brush dry out as a fire burns uphill. Winds also carry away moisture as they sweep over the fire, so the unburned fuels will ignite more easily. The steeper the hill, the faster a fire will move. Houses built at the top of a hill are more likely to catch fire than houses built on flat land. They are also more likely to be struck by lightning, which tends to hit the highest things standing.

Types of Wildfires

Firefighters classify wildfires into several groups, according to how they spread and the kinds of things they burn. The main types are ground fires, surface fires, crown fires, and spot fires.

Ground fires. These wildfires may start in the packed-down layer of dry leaves, rotted wood, and other dried-out fuel on the forest floor. This layer is called litter. The fire spreads into the buried part of the litter, which is not in direct contact with air. Ground fires move slowly along the forest floor because their air supply is so limited. They can produce a lot of smoke, but there may not be flames. Ground fires may lead to surface fires.

Surface fires. These are wildfires that burn grasses, bushes, and fallen branches and trees. They spread quickly along the forest floor because the plant life is surrounded by air. Surface fires produce more flames than ground fires. The flames may become taller and hotter if there is a lot of fuel around. Flames of surface fires may quickly climb small trees. This kind of fire can soon turn into a crown fire.

Crown fires. Occurring in the treetops, crown fires are the most dangerous type of wildfires. They are fueled by the winds. The winds supply them with more oxygen. As the fires grow, they can spread to shrubs or trees that are higher than one meter (four feet) tall. Winds can easily spread the flames from one treetop to the next. Crown fires can become extremely hot and are very difficult to control. These fires are often called firestorms.

Spot fires. High winds and crown fires can lead to spot fires. Spot fires happen when the wind carries embers to other areas and starts new fires. Thus, new fires can start on the other side of a river or road from the original fire.

WHAT CAUSES WILDFIRES?

In October 1871

Chicago, Illinois, had one of the worst fires in United States history. Dry weather and strong winds helped spread the fire. It spread quickly, burning the wooden houses, shops, barns, warehouses, and roads. In the end, the famous Great Chicago Fire killed up to three hundred people, left a hundred thousand homeless, and destroyed thousands of houses and buildings.[1] According to popular stories, this disastrous fire started in a barn when "Mrs. O'Leary's cow" kicked over an oil lantern. But today historians believe this fire most likely started when someone carelessly dropped a lit match or cigarette.

A bolt of lightning has sparked a wildfire in Idaho.

People and Fires

Most wildfires are started by people's careless actions. As seen in the 2007 Southern California wildfires, just a single match smoldering in dry grass can turn into a huge, frightening disaster.

Cigarette smoking is involved in many fires. Smokers may carelessly toss away a cigarette while walking or driving by a field or forest. If the cigarette is still smoldering, it could ignite dry grass or brush.

Why Are Fireworks So Dangerous?

Fireworks are very dangerous because they contain gunpowder. When they explode, they get really hot. People can lose their fingers if fireworks go off in their hands. If they set off fireworks in a wooded area, it could start a wildfire.

Also, campers may not put their campfires out completely. Winds can stir up the embers and restart a campfire, or they may blow the hot embers into nearby areas, starting new fires there.

Some wildfires are caused by arson. This means that someone ignited the fire on purpose. Fire officials discovered that a few of the 2007 Southern California fires were due to arson.

A firefighter tries to control a wildfire breakout in Eugene, Oregon, by lighting a backfire: a small fire that stops the big one by burning up its fuel supply.

Lightning Strikes

Every year, thousands of wildfires are started by lightning strikes. Lightning is a form of electricity. It can release heat as hot as the sun—up to as much as 30,000 degrees Celsius (about 54,000 degrees Fahrenheit)! If a lightning bolt shoots out of a thunder-cloud and strikes a tree, a house, or some other burnable object, it can start a fire. In many wilderness areas in the United States, lightning is a common cause of wildfires.

Electrical Problems

A fire can start when a house or building has old or bad electrical wiring. When electrical cords are worn, the wires may come into contact with each other and short out, creating sparks. Plugging too many electrical devices into an outlet may heat up the wires until they catch fire. A fire may start inside the wall, smolder for a while, and then spread through the house. When houses are close together or close to dry fields or woods, a house fire can turn into a wildfire.

These trees catch fire as a result of lava flow from Hawaii's Kilauea volcano.

Natural Disasters

Earthquakes, tornadoes, and hurricanes can lead to fires. For example, during the 1906 San Francisco earthquake, much of the city was destroyed not by the earthquake itself, but mostly by the fires that broke out. The earthquake broke gas lines, which exploded, starting fires all over the city. These fires raged on for four days. Water lines had also broken, and firefighters could not get water to put out the fires.

Slash and Burn

In some parts of the world, such as the rain forests, people burn down forests to clear land for farming. In what is known as slash-and-burn farming, farmers cut down trees and burn the tree trunks. The ash that is left helps provide for good crops. This benefit is only temporary, though. Without the tree roots to hold water in the soil, the ash is soon washed away by rain. The world is losing its rain forests due to these practices.

Natural disasters can also break power lines or utility poles. The fallen power lines send out sparks that can start fires in nearby grass or litter.

When a volcano erupts, it spits out hot ashes into the air. It may also ooze lava over the side of the mountain. The hot lava can set fire to grasses, trees, houses, or anything else in its path. Hot ashes can also ignite fires when they land on burnable objects.

Prescribed Fire

Not all wildfires are unwanted. In some cases, firefighters purposely start fires themselves in certain wooded areas. Why? Fires are a natural part of a forest's life cycle. They clear away dead trees, shrubs, and litter so that new seedlings will have room and light to grow. Fires also help recycle nutrients. The ashes of the old trees and bushes mix with the soil and help feed the new growth. When fires don't occur naturally, burnable materials build up. They provide fuel for wildfires.

The fires that forestry workers start are called prescribed fire, or prescribed burns. The people who start them are professionals. They make sure that the areas that burn are far enough away from neighborhoods. Prescribed burns actually help keep the forests healthy and prevent unwanted fires.

THE DANGERS OF WILDFIRES

5

Every year, TV and radio stations feature news stories about wildfires. These fires become big news because they are huge and spread quickly. Meanwhile, thousands of small wildfires happen every year that people don't hear about.

Records show that about 64,000 unwanted wildfires occur in the United States every year. Many of them are small and not too serious, but altogether, wildfires may burn as much as 4.3 million acres a year.[1]

Wildfires destroy more than 900 homes every year.[2] They can be dangerous to people and pets. They can also have a serious effect on the environment and the wildlife that lives there.

Plants and Wildlife

When a fire sweeps through a forest, it can damage grasses, bushes, and trees. It may even burn everything down to the ground. It can change a whole landscape. But plants and animals have ways of coping with wildfires.

Some animals may run away from the fire. Birds can fly away. Animals that burrow hide out in underground tunnels until the fire passes. The soil helps shield them from the heat. Tunnels just five to eight centimeters (two to three inches) below the surface are safe from a fire.

Plants obviously can't fly or run away. But some of them can protect themselves from wildfires in other ways. For example, Western larch trees have very thick bark that can survive surface fires. Some bushes resprout from roots after a fire has destroyed their branches. Most eucalyptus trees grow new branches from their trunks.

* It's a Fact! *
Some plants may sprout or bloom only after a wildfire. The cones of jack pines in the Rocky Mountains, for example, are sealed by a waxy substance. The heat of a fire melts the wax. Then the seeds in the pinecone can fall to the forest floor and sprout in the ash from the fire.

People and Pets

When a house catches fire, everyone in it is in great danger—both people and their pets. A fire can heat up objects very quickly. For example, a doorknob might be too hot to touch when a person tries to turn it. Curtains can quickly go up in flames. Many people get burned when they try to get out of a house that is on fire. Burns can be extremely painful. Heat from the fire can ignite the outer skin layers or even destroy deeper tissues. Burns need immediate medical attention. People can die in a fire from the intense heat if they cannot get to safety in time.

However, burns are not the main cause of death in fires. From 50 to 80 percent of deaths in fires are the result of smoke inhalation,

The image on the left was taken before wildfires struck California in October 2007. On the right, the same scene shows bushes with leaves and branches burned away. (The pink color is due to chemicals sprayed to stop the fire.)

or breathing in smoke.[3] Smoke is a mixture of hot particles and gases. The smoke's heat can burn the lining of a person's breathing passages and lungs. Some of the chemicals in smoke can make the throat swell up and cause severe coughing and breathing problems. Carbon monoxide, carbon dioxide, and other gases in smoke prevent the cells from picking up or using oxygen, which could be fatal. Breathing pure oxygen through a mask or breathing tube is a treatment for smoke inhalation.

Pollution

Wildfires pour tons of soot, ash, and other combustion products into the atmosphere. The soot and ash in the smoke can change

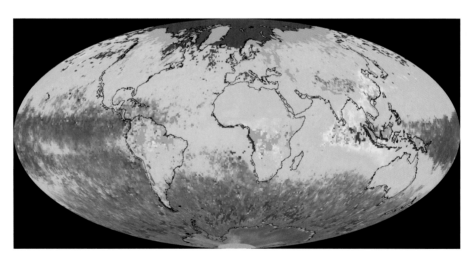

This satellite image shows the concentration of carbon monoxide (CO) in Earth's atmosphere, ranging from very little (blue) to average (green) to high (red). High levels of CO are an indication of wildfire activity.

the weather in the areas around it. They lead to clouds and storms. Meanwhile, hot air rising from the fire carries carbon monoxide and other harmful gases high into the atmosphere. Winds may take them far away. After the record-breaking wildfires in Alaska in 2004, for example, researchers found pollutants from the fires as far away as Europe.

How Hot Is It Inside a Burning House?

The heat from a fire is enough to kill someone. At floor level, the room temperature can be around 38 degrees Celsius (about 100 degrees Fahrenheit). But at eye level, the temperature can reach more than 315 degrees Celsius (about 600 degrees Fahrenheit)! Temperatures higher than 49 degrees Celsius (120 degrees Fahrenheit) are hot enough to burn skin.

STAYING
SAFE

6

More and more people

are building their homes near forests, rural areas, or mountains. That means more and more people will be threatened by wildfires. But unlike other natural disasters, most wildfires can be prevented.

Wildfires can happen anywhere, so everybody should practice fire safety. It is important to know what to do in case of a fire emergency to keep you and your family safe.

Practice Fire Safety

Do you practice fire safety?

- Never play with matches, cigarette lighters, or candles.
- Be careful handling gasoline, chemical cleaning fluids, and starter fluids for outdoor grills. They can flare up suddenly

A fireman teaches elementary school students how to avoid smoke inhalation while escaping a fire by dropping to the floor.

Smokey Bear

Smokey Bear has become an American symbol to help fight wildfires. You have probably seen Smokey Bear signs alongside highways. They give wildfire warnings that may read "low," "moderate," or "high." These warnings describe the risk for wildfires in the area. For example, hot, dry weather indicates a high risk for wildfires. That means people should be extra careful.

if there is an open flame or spark nearby.

- Fireworks are another big fire hazard. They are not toys and should be handled only by professionals.

Fireproofing outside your house can also help. For example, clear away fallen branches, leaves, and brush from around your house. They can fuel a fire. Keep a safety zone around your house, with bushes and trees at least nine meters (about thirty feet) away. Plants that store water in their stems or leaves, such as ice plants, can be planted closer. They resist fire and may help protect the house.

What to Do in a Fire

Would you know what to do in a fire? You should practice fire drills with your parents. Find the safest ways to get out of your house.

Keep a disaster kit handy in case of an emergency. It should include a supply of food and water, a first aid kit, a flashlight and

An illustration of Smokey Bear accompanies this sign warning of fire danger in Augusta, Montana.

batteries, a battery-operated radio, protective clothing and shoes, blankets, and special items for babies, the elderly, and pets. Store these supplies in easy-to-carry backpacks or duffel bags.

Listen for wildfire warnings on the radio or TV, and follow the instructions. If the local officials say to go find a safe shelter, don't waste time. Leave as quickly as you can. Don't stop to gather personal belongings. There may be only enough time for you and your family to escape.

What Should You Do About Your Pets If There Is a Wildfire?

If possible, do not leave your pets behind if you have to evacuate. They will not have a good chance of surviving on their own.

Plan ahead. Emergency shelters will not usually take in pets. So look for hotels and motels outside your local area that will accept pets. Make a list of animal boarders and veterinary offices that might be able to keep animals in case of an emergency. Your pets should all have collars and identification tags.

If your house catches fire, follow your planned escape route. But remember, heat and smoke rise, so crawl along the floor. If your clothes catch on fire, remember these important words: *stop*, *drop*, and *roll*. That means *stop* what you're doing, *drop* to the floor, and *roll* over. This should put out the fire and save you from further harm. It may even save your life.

Fighting Fires

The best way to fight wildfires is to find them when they are still small. Fire lookouts are people who watch for smoke or flames in the national forests. They phone or radio in the fire's location to firefighting officials. The lookouts are stationed in towers high enough to give a view of a large area.

Thousands of specially trained firefighters risk their lives to bring wildfires under control. Up-to-date weather reports and forecasts from the National Weather Service help guide their efforts. The firefighters use several main methods.

Hotshots are teams of twenty people who work to build a firebreak around the fire to stop it from spreading. A firebreak is a narrow piece of land that is stripped of brush, grasses, and other burnable materials. The hotshots use shovels, axes, and chainsaws to clear the firebreak.

Smokejumpers parachute out of planes to get to fires in out-of-the-way areas. They fight fires that are still small, using the same methods as the hotshots.

Fighting Fire With Fire

Sometimes firefighters start fires to stop a wildfire. These small fires, called backfires, move toward the wildfire, destroying the fuel in its path. There is nothing to feed on in the backfired area, so the wildfire stops spreading.

Ground crews may also spray water and fire retardants to put out fires. The chemicals in a fire retardant help smother and cool down a fire.

Airplanes and helicopters often help the ground crews. They carry water and fire retardants to dump on a spreading wildfire. Helicopters dump water bombs from buckets that can hold hundreds of gallons. The fire retardants used are a pink, gooey substance, which is sometimes called sky Jell-o.

A plane drops flame retardant on the northern edge of a wildfire near Crown King, Arizona, on June 30, 2008.

The best way to fight fires, however, is to prevent them. Since most wildfires are caused by people's actions, everyone can help by being extra careful when using fire.

Wildfires are natural disasters that don't have to happen. As Smokey Bear says: "Only you can prevent wildfires."

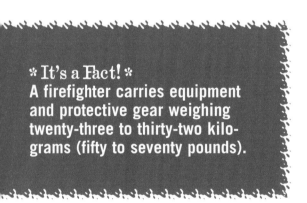

* It's a Fact! *
A firefighter carries equipment and protective gear weighing twenty-three to thirty-two kilograms (fifty to seventy pounds).

CHAPTER NOTES

CHAPTER 1. AGUA DULCE BURNS

1. "Facts About Wind and Wildfires," *Weather.com: Weather Ready*, 2008, <http://www.weather.com/ready/fire/facts.html> (August 28, 2008).

2. "Outdoor Fires," *U.S. Fire Administration Topical Fire Research Series*, January 2002, <http://www.usfa.dhs.gov/downloads/pdf/tfrs/v2i19-508.pdf> (August 28, 2008).

3. William H. Welch, Patrick O'Driscoll, and Chris Woodward, "Shifting Winds May Help California Firefighters," *USA Today*, October 23, 2007, <http://www.usatoday.com/weather/wildfires/2007-10-23-wildfires_N.htm> (August 29, 2008).

4. "Police: Boy Playing With Matches Started 38,000-Acre Fire," *CNN.com*, October 31, 2007, <http://www.cnn.com/2007/US/10/31/fire.california/index.html> (January 14, 2008).

5. Associated Press, "Firefighters Make Progress Against Blaze Near Malibu," *CNN.com*, November 24, 2007, <http://www.cnn.com/2007/US/11/24/california.wildfire/index.html> (January 22, 2008).

6. Ibid.

CHAPTER 2. WHAT IS FIRE?

1. "This Is Fire! A Factsheet on the Nature of Fire," *U.S. Fire Administration*, March 2006, <http://usfa.dhs.gov/downloads/pdf/fswy6.pdf> (January 25, 2008).

CHAPTER 4. WHAT CAUSES WILDFIRES?

1. "The Chicago Fire," *Chicago Historical Society*, 1999, <http://www.chicagohs.org/history/fire.html> (February 11, 2008).

CHAPTER 5. THE DANGERS OF WILDFIRES

1. "NIMO Feasibility and Implementation Plan," *National Incident Management Organization*, November 2005, <http://boisenimo.imtcenter.net/main/DocumentLink.aspx?ID=246> (February 11, 2008).

2. "Prevention: Your Home," *SmokeyBear.com*, n.d., <http://www.smokeybear.com/home.asp> (February 11, 2008).

3. Christopher P. Holstege, M.D., "Smoke Inhalation," *eMedicineHealth*, reviewed October 18, 2007, <http://www.emedicinehealth.com/smoke_inhalation/article_em.htm> (February 13, 2008).

GLOSSARY

arson—Illegally setting a fire on purpose.

ash—A powdery gray solid left after burning. It contains all the unburnable minerals in the fuel.

backfires—Small fires set by firefighters as a way to fight wildfires. Backfires keep a wildfire from spreading by destroying the fuel in its path.

brush—A thick growth of bushes sometimes accompanied by small trees.

chemical reaction—A process in which substances change into other substances.

combustible—Able to burn.

combustion—Burning; a fast chemical reaction that uses oxygen to produce heat and light.

conduction—Passage of heat from a fire through objects in direct contact with the fire.

convection—Rising of heated air and falling of cool air to take its place. The constant movement of air helps spread a fire.

crown fire—A dangerous fire that occurs in the treetops and spreads quickly with the help of winds.

embers—The remains of fuel that have not burned completely.

firebreak—A strip of land from which all plant life and brush has been cleared so that a fire doesn't have any fuel to burn.

fire lookout—A person who watches for smoke or flames in national forests and phones or radios in the fire's location to firefighting officials.

fire retardant—A substance that helps keep a fire from spreading.

flammable—See combustible.

fuel—A burnable substance.

friction—Rubbing of one surface against another, which generates heat.

ground fire—A fire that burns dry leaves, sticks, and other plant life on the forest floor. It moves slowly and produces more smoke than flames.

hotshot—A twenty-person team that clears fuel from a strip of land around a wildfire to stop it from spreading.

ignite—Start a fire.

ignition point—The temperature at which a fuel starts burning.

lightning—A sudden release of electricity within or from a storm cloud, producing a brilliant flash of light and generating intense heat.

litter—The packed-down layer of dry leaves, rotted wood, and other dried-out fuel on the forest floor.

matter—Anything that has weight and takes up space.

prescribed burn—A fire set by forestry experts under selected weather conditions to eliminate a buildup of forest fuels that could lead to uncontrolled fires. (Also called prescribed fire.)

radiation—Spreading of heat from a fire outward in all directions.

smoke—A mixture of burning gases and tiny carbon particles.

smoke inhalation—Breathing in smoke.

smokejumpers—Firefighters who parachute out of planes to get to fires in out-of-the-way areas.

smoldering—A slow burning, which can produce a lot of smoke but no visible flames.

spot fires—New fires started by hot ash or embers carried by wind from a wildfire farther away.

surface fire—A fires that burns grasses, bushes, and fallen branches and trees. It may spread to small trees.

wildfire—A rapidly spreading fire, especially in a wilderness or rural area.

FURTHER READING

Costain, Meredith. *Science Chapters: Devouring Flames: The Story of Forest Fires*. Washington, D.C.: National Geographic Children's Books, 2006.

Morrison, Taylor. *Wildfire*. New York: Houghton Mifflin Company, 2006.

Peluso, Beth A. *The Charcoal Forest: How Fires Help Animals and Plants*. Missoula, Minn.: Mountain Press Publishing Company, 2007.

Trumbauer, Lisa. *Forest Fires*. New York: Franklin Watts, 2005.

Woods, Michael and Mary Woods. *Fires*. Minneapolis, Minn.: Lerner Publications Company, 2007.

INTERNET ADDRESSES

"Only You Can Prevent Wildfires," *SmokeyBear.com*, <http://www.smokey bear.com/> (February 14, 2008). [*A fun, animated Web site with lots of information about wildfires, how to prevent them, and a special page all about firefighters. This site also includes a special kids' page with stories, activities, and facts about the forest and wildfires.*]

"USFA Kids," *U.S. Fire Administration for Kids*, <http://www.usfa.dhs.gov/kids/flash.shtm> (February 14, 2008). [*Kid-friendly site with information about home fire safety, smoke alarms, and escaping from a fire; also includes quizzes and fun activities.*]

"Wildfires," *National Geographic for Kids*, <http://magma.nationalgeographic.com/ngexplorer/0111/adventures/> (February 14, 2008). [*Information on wildfires, quizzes, and photos and audio of firefighters in action.*]

INDEX